George Chan
Dream Farms / Traumfarmen

Introduction / Einführung:
Fernando García-Dory

dOCUMENTA (13)

HATJE
CANTZ

Fernando García-Dory

Dream Farms
The Lost Path: Learning from George Chan's Legacy

I want all of you to know how I appreciate your efforts,
and have not given up yet.
—George Chan, open letter, 2007

In the current social, environmental, and economic crisis, a search
for alternative systems for every domain of life seems urgent. Many
scientists and experts have formulated such alternatives, which now
work as lighthouses for other projects that emulate them, joining
in the collective effort for a more sustainable and equitable model
of society. Among these systems are agroecological approaches
such as permaculture—systems modeled on the structures found
in nature and involving input from fields such as architecture, agri-
culture, and energy and waste management, in a holistic approach
based on ecosystem dynamics and aiming for practical solutions
for sustainable development.

Professor George Chan has been a pioneer in this field and is
considered a world expert on the sustainable recycling of waste and
on agroecological systems. Now, at the age of eighty-eight and in
delicate health, he is the guardian of an immense body of knowledge
and experience that will be lost unless it is left as a legacy for present
and future generations.

Born in Mauritius in 1923, Chan served in the British Colonial
Army from 1942 to 1945 and then went on to study engineering in
London on an army scholarship. After working in Port Louis, Mauritius, he tested and developed his ideas all over the world, employed
by the South Pacific Commission in New Caledonia and later by the
Commonwealth of the Northern Mariana Islands (CNMI), where he
witnessed the problems of poverty, sanitation, and lack of development

on many groups of small isolated islands. In 1983, having worked with peasants in China in order to learn their techniques in ancient farming systems, he commented in his autobiographical notes: "We learnt many lessons on HOW to do so Much with so Little, and WHY we should Recycle all wastes and residues, which were resources before. I could have worked 5 more years in a cushy job in CNMI, but I chose to go to China as a volunteer not only to teach, but also to learn as well. What an education it was!" Afterward, Chan continued developing projects and leading courses around the world, in countries including the U.S.A., Brazil, and Japan, and working with the Folkecenter for Renewable Energy in Denmark and Zero Emissions Research and Initiatives (ZERI), two major research-and-development centers for sustainability strategies. Sadly, an accident some years ago and a resulting brain operation put a stop to his public scientific activity. He now lives a reclusive life in Mauritius.

The model that Chan came up with after years of research and development was the Integrated Farming and Waste Management System (IFWMS), which he hoped would be implemented extensively among farmers and smallholders to boost productivity and ensure a fair income for all. It involves a sustainable cycle in which matter and energy circulate through different stages, dramatically increasing yields. This revolutionary model—named Dream Farms—remains, however, largely unknown.

I became deeply interested not only in the content of Chan's work but in the way in which he has explained it; not only in the body of theory and practice but in its form; not only in the scientist but in the person. Three years ago I made contact with Preben Maegaard, director of the Folkecenter for Renewable Energy and an old friend and collaborator of Chan's. Together with Gunter Pauli from the ZERI, he encouraged me to recover as much as possible from Chan's legacy with the aim of publishing a book based on his materials. When I met Chan at the old people's home where he lives near Port Louis, he could hardly speak, so we were not able to communicate in depth, and unfortunately he could not help me understand, as someone without specialist knowledge of waste-management engineering, some of the crucial technical details that make his system operative. Unable to stand up and leave his bed, he could not see the rusting merchant ships grounded on the beach beneath his window.

Readers will be astonished by the huge accumulation of knowledge demonstrated in this notebook, which nevertheless contains a very small portion of Chan's materials. Those that I have selected give an idea of IFWMS, rather than constituting the comprehensive book it deserves. All designs, slides, and text layouts are presented as Chan envisioned them.

The pictures here are of systems from all corners of the world: DIY digesters, waste basins, and fish ponds in tropical lands—warm, wet, remote places, where economies are limited. Inventiveness and the wise use of biological processes along with recycled industrial components and cheap building materials together constitute an "intermediate" or "soft" technology—one that is valid for an increasingly populated planet with limited resources; a technological and creative investment, this time, for the rest of mankind.

The system that Chan designed and perfected over the years extends the life and utility of those substances deemed to be "waste" products by modern industrial farming systems. Such matter mutates through different states—growth, transformation, decay—until it is considered waste, irremediably without energy or use, and it ends up in awkward piles or buried underground. But in fact the concept of waste is not definitive; it is directly related to a civilization's level of knowledge at any given point of its technological development. Chan's work is strictly negentropic, that is, negatively entropic, because it allows further complex structural processes and configurations, partially reversing the universal tendency to dissipation. In this sense, his proposal could be compared to alchemy: a formula to transform a useless substance into a precious and coveted material. This is the dream of humanity. So far, it is a formula that remains blurry, with some lost element or step. It is a distant vision in the dreams of an aged intelligence, exhausted, weakened, and confined.

During one of my visits, in a lucid moment, Chan declared to me: "I have dedicated my life to helping the poor and the neediest of this world to transform their waste into wealth. . . . And here I am, almost ninety years later, forgotten and left in an old people's home." I was touched by this expression of the imbalance and fragility of life. It made me realize the challenges lying ahead to further develop a life of research and to keep it connected to the achievement of a lived life, the one of George Chan. It brings to mind Robert Musil, who once wrote: "The most surprising aspect of monuments is that we never see them. There is nothing in this world as invisible as a monument." These incomplete, fragmented notes are a first step in keeping alive the work of Professor Chan.

Fernando García-Dory (b. 1978) is an artist and agroecologist living between Madrid, Berlin, and the northern Spanish mountains.

The author would like to thank Professors Maegaard and Pauli for the confidence they placed in him, Folkecenter, Denmark, for supporting the mission, J. Narvaez for his assistance, as well as Chus Martínez for her visionary stake in this project, and Carolyn Christov-Bakargiev for creating the possibility to reflect on George Chan's life and work.

Fernando García-Dory

Traumfarmen
Der verlorene Weg: von George Chans Vermächtnis lernen

*Ich möchte Euch alle wissen lassen, wie sehr ich Eure Bemühungen
schätze, und dass ich noch nicht aufgegeben habe.*
– George Chan, offener Brief, 2007

In der aktuellen Gesellschafts-, Umwelt- und Wirtschaftskrise
erscheint die Suche nach alternativen Systemen für jeden Lebens-
bereich dringend geboten. Viele Wissenschaftler und Experten
haben solche Alternativen vorgestellt, die jetzt als Leuchttürme für
andere Projekte fungieren, die ihnen nacheifern und sich damit dem
kollektiven Bemühen um ein nachhaltigeres und gerechteres Gesell-
schaftsmodell anschließen. Zu diesen Systemen zählen agrarökologische Ansätze wie die Permakultur – Verfahren, die sich in einem
ganzheitlichen Ansatz, der auf der Dynamik von Ökosystemen
basiert und praktische Lösungen für eine nachhaltige Entwicklung
anstrebt, an den in der Natur vorhandenen Strukturen orientieren
und Kenntnisse aus Bereichen wie Architektur, Land-, Energie- und
Abfallwirtschaft nutzen.

Professor George Chan ist ein Pionier auf diesem Gebiet und gilt
als weltweiter Experte für das nachhaltige Wiederaufbereiten von
Abfällen und für agrarökologische Systeme. Heute, mit 88 Jahren
und bei fragiler Gesundheit, ist er der Hüter eines gewaltigen
Wissens- und Erfahrungsschatzes, der verloren gehen wird, wenn es
nicht gelingt, ihn als Vermächtnis für heutige und zukünftige Gene-
rationen zu erhalten.

Der 1923 auf Mauritius geborene Chan diente von 1942 bis
1945 in der Britischen Kolonialarmee und studierte anschließend
mit einem Armeestipendium in London Ingenieurswissenschaften.
Nachdem er in Port Louis (Mauritius) gearbeitet hatte, testete und

entwickelte er seine Ideen in der ganzen Welt als Angestellter der South Pacific Commission in Neukaledonien und später des Commonwealth der Nördlichen Marianen (CNMI). Dabei wurde er auf den zahlreichen isolierten Inselgruppen Zeuge von Problemen wie Armut, fehlenden sanitären Anlagen und mangelhafter Entwicklung. 1983, als er in China mit Bauern zusammengearbeitet hatte, um die Techniken ihrer alten Landwirtschaftssysteme kennenzulernen, schrieb er in seinen autobiografischen Aufzeichnungen: »Wir erhielten so viele Lektionen darin, WIE man mit so *wenig* so *viel* machen kann, und WARUM wir alle Abfälle und Reste, die vorher Rohstoffe waren, *recyceln* sollen. Ich hätte noch 5 Jahre in einem bequemen Job beim CNMI verbringen können, aber ich beschloss, als Freiwilliger nach China zu gehen, nicht nur um zu lehren, sondern auch um zu lernen. Was für eine Ausbildung das war!« Danach entwickelte Chan weiter weltweit Projekte, etwa in Ländern wie den USA, Brasilien und Japan, hielt Lehrveranstaltungen ab und arbeitete mit dem Folkecenter für erneuerbare Energie in Dänemark sowie mit Zero Emissions Research and Initiatives (ZERI) zusammen, zwei bedeutenden Forschungs- und Entwicklungszentren für Nachhaltigkeitsstrategien. Leider bereiteten vor einigen Jahren ein Unfall und die anschließende Gehirnoperation seiner öffentlichen wissenschaftlichen Tätigkeit ein Ende. Chan lebt heute zurückgezogen auf Mauritius.

Das Modell, mit dem Chan nach Jahren der Forschung und Entwicklung aufwartete, war das Integrated Farming and Waste Management System [Integriertes Land- und Abfallwirtschaftssystem] (IFWMS), von dem er hoffte, dass Landwirte und Kleinbauern es ausgedehnt anwenden würden, um ihre Produktivität zu erhöhen und ein faires Einkommen für alle zu gewährleisten. Es umfasst einen nachhaltigen Kreislauf, bei dem Materie und Energie verschiedene Stufen durchlaufen und die Erträge ganz erheblich gesteigert werden. Dieses revolutionäre Modell namens »Dream Farms« ist jedoch relativ unbekannt geblieben.

Ich begann mich nicht nur sehr für die inhaltliche Seite von Chans Werk zu interessieren, sondern auch für die Art und Weise, wie er dieses Werk erklärte, nicht nur für die Theorie und Praxis an sich, sondern auch für ihre Gestalt, nicht nur für den Wissenschaftler, sondern auch für die Person. Vor drei Jahren nahm ich Kontakt mit Preben Maegaard auf, der Direktor des Folkecenter für erneuerbare Energie und ein alter Freund und Mitarbeiter von Chan ist. Gemeinsam mit Gunter Pauli von ZERI ermutigte er mich, so viel wie möglich von Chans Vermächtnis zusammenzutragen, um auf der Grundlage seiner Unterlagen ein Buch zu veröffentlichen. Als ich Chan in dem Altersheim traf, in dem er in der Nähe von Port

Louis lebt, war es ihm kaum möglich zu sprechen, so dass wir keine tiefgehende Unterhaltung führen konnten; leider war er daher auch nicht in der Lage, mir, der ich über kein Spezialwissen hinsichtlich der ingenieurstechnischen Aspekte der Abfallwirtschaft verfüge, beim Verständnis einiger der entscheidenden technischen Details zu helfen, die dafür verantwortlich sind, dass seine Methode funktioniert. Außerstande, aufzustehen und sein Bett zu verlassen, konnte er die verrostenden Handelsschiffe, die unter seinem Fenster am Strand lagen, nicht sehen.

Die Leser werden über die immense Wissensansammlung staunen, die in diesem Notizbuch vorgestellt wird, obwohl es nur einen Bruchteil von Chans Dokumenten enthält. Die von mir ausgewählten Fragmente vermitteln lediglich eine bescheidene Vorstellung des IFWMS, ersetzen jedoch keineswegs die umfassende Publikation, die es verdiente. Sämtliche Entwürfe, Dias und Text-Layouts werden so präsentiert, wie Chan sie vorgesehen hatte.

Die Bilder hier stammen von Systemen aus allen Winkeln der Welt: Do-it-yourself-Biokonverter, Abfallbecken und Fischteiche in tropischen Ländern – warmen, feuchten, entlegenen Orten mit eingeschränkten Volkswirtschaften. Erfindungsreichtum und der kluge Einsatz biologischer Prozesse neben recycelten Industriekomponenten und billigem Baumaterial bilden gemeinsam eine »intermediäre« oder »weiche« Technologie, die einem immer bevölkerungsreicheren Planeten, der aber nur über begrenzte Ressourcen verfügt, gerecht wird – eine technologische und kreative Investition, diesmal, für den Rest der Menschheit.

Das System, das Chan entwarf und über die Jahre perfektionierte, verlängert das Leben und den Nutzwert jener Substanzen, die von den modernen industrialisierten Landwirtschaftssystemen als »Abfall«-Produkte angesehen werden. Diese Stoffe durchlaufen verschiedene Phasen – Wachstum, Verwandlung, Verfall –, bis sie schließlich als definitiv nicht weiter verwertbarer, energiefreier Abfall gelten, der auf unansehnlichen Haufen endet oder in der Erde vergraben wird. Tatsächlich aber ist das Konzept Abfall nicht für alle Zeiten endgültig definiert, sondern steht in direkter Beziehung zum Wissensniveau einer Kultur zu einem bestimmten Zeitpunkt ihrer technologischen Entwicklung. Chans Werk ist streng negentropisch, also negativ entropisch, da es weitere komplexe strukturelle Prozesse und Konfigurationen zulässt und die allgemeine Tendenz zur Verschwendung teilweise umkehrt. In diesem Sinne lässt sich sein Vorschlag mit der Alchemie vergleichen: eine Formel, mit der sich eine nutzlose Substanz in ein wertvolles und begehrtes Material verwandeln lässt. Das ist der Traum der Menschheit. Doch bislang bleibt diese Formel vage, irgendein Element oder Schritt fehlt darin.

Es handelt sich um eine entfernte Vision in den Träumen einer gealterten – erschöpften, geschwächten und gefangenen – Intelligenz.

Bei einem meiner Besuche sagte Chan in einem lichten Moment zu mir: »Ich habe mein Leben der Aufgabe gewidmet, den Armen und Bedürftigsten dieser Welt dabei zu helfen, ihren Abfall in Reichtum zu verwandeln. [...] Und hier bin ich, fast neunzig Jahre später, vergessen und verlassen in einem Altersheim.« Mich rührte dieser Ausdruck der Unausgewogenheit und Zerbrechlichkeit des Lebens. Er veranschaulichte mir die vor uns liegenden Herausforderungen, ein der Forschung gewidmetes Leben weiterzuentwickeln und seine Verbindung mit den Errungenschaften eines gelebten Lebens, des Lebens von George Chan, aufrechtzuerhalten. Man fühlt sich an Robert Musil erinnert, der einmal schrieb: »[…] das Auffallendste an Denkmälern ist nämlich, daß man sie nicht bemerkt. Es gibt nichts auf der Welt, was so unsichtbar wäre wie Denkmäler.« Diese unvollständigen, fragmentarischen Aufzeichnungen sind ein erster Schritt, um das Werk Professor Chans am Leben zu erhalten.

Fernando García-Dory (geb. 1978) ist Künstler und Agrarökologe und lebt zwischen Madrid, Berlin und den Bergen Nordspaniens.

Der Verfasser dankt den Professoren Maegaard und Pauli für das Vertrauen, das sie in ihn gesetzt haben, dem Folkecenter, Dänemark, für die Unterstützung dieser Arbeit, J. Narvaez für seine Assistenz, Chus Martínez für ihren visionären Anteil an diesem Projekt und Carolyn Christov-Bakargiev dafür, dass sie die Möglichkeit geschaffen hat, über George Chans Leben und Werk nachzudenken.

INTEGRATED DIGESTER-BASIN-POND-FIELD RECYCLING SYSTEMS

Prof. George L. CHAN

Complete **RECYCLING** of **ALL** Resources
For Food **Sustainability** & Ecological **Balance**

The **FUTURE** in the Whole World will Consist
of a National System of **LOCAL** Integrated
FOOD and **WASTE** Recycling Networks

WASTE NOT, WANT NOT!
Prof. George L. CHAN, Environmental Engineering Specialist

WASTENOT01
chanbioDec02

The most **important** thing we all
learn from **Nature** is that:

MATTER CANNOT BE CREATED NOR DESTROYED!

Yet what the **modern** world does all
the time is to **create** 'NEW' things
and
leave more **WASTES** to be
destroyed!

50m³ SEDIMENTATION TANK
for Single Integrated Farm with Pigs

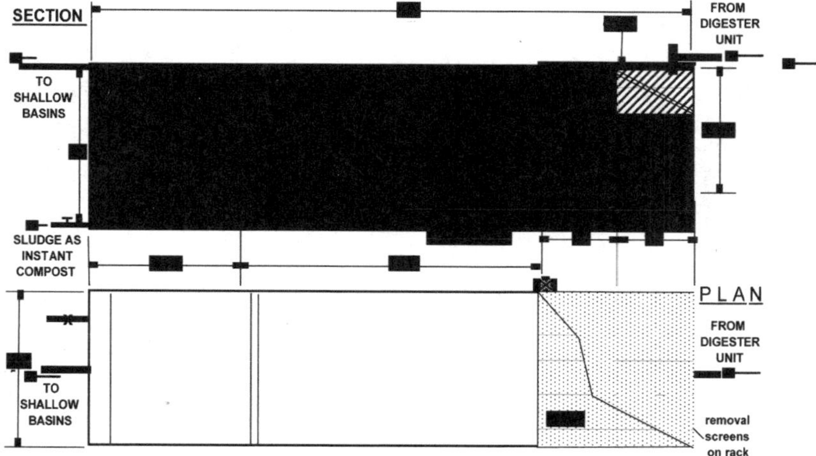

WASTE NOT, WANT NOT!

IT IS **AGAINST** NATURE, which already has its own <u>PROCESSES</u> and <u>LAWS</u>.

We cannot **change** Nature, which has its own **'wasteful'** ways but it also provides its own 'natural' **recycling** solutions.

We can **enhance** Nature's processes by **improving** the **recycling** with ingenuity.

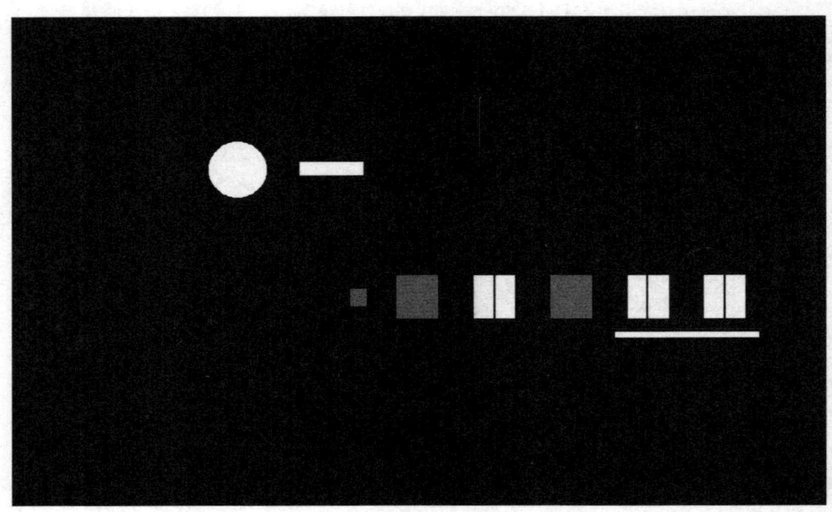

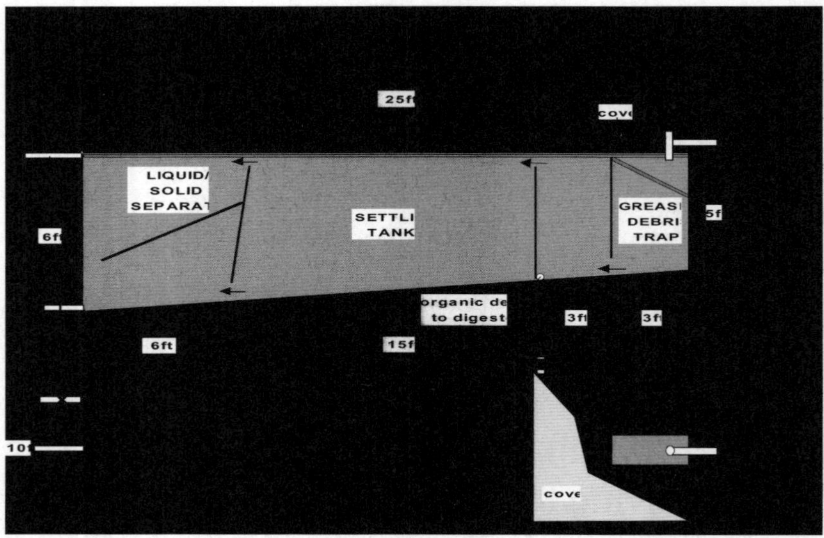

25ft
cove
LIQUID/
SOLID
SEPARAT
SETTLI
TANK
GREASI
DEBRI
TRAP
5f
6ft
6ft
15f
organic de
to digest
3ft
3ft
10f
cove

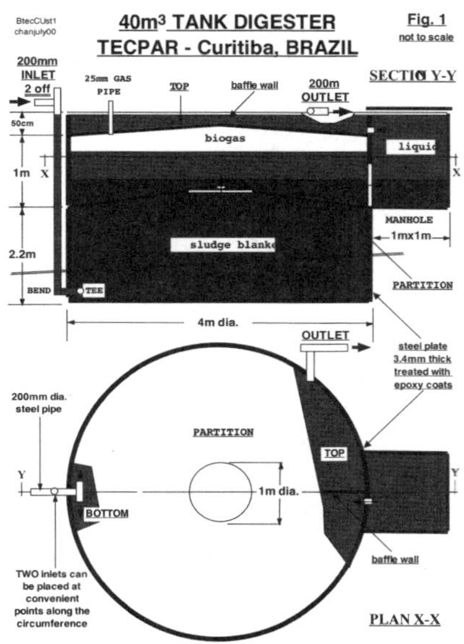

BtecCUst1
chanjuly00
40m³ TANK DIGESTER
TECPAR - Curitiba, BRAZIL
Fig. 1
not to scale
200mm INLET 2 off
25mm GAS PIPE
TOP
baffle wall
200m OUTLET
SECTION Y-Y
50cm
biogas
liquid
1m X
X
2.2m
sludge blanke
MANHOLE
1mx1m
PARTITION
BEND
TEE
4m dia.
OUTLET
steel plate 3.4mm thick treated with epoxy coats
200mm dia. steel pipe
PARTITION
TOP
Y
Y
BOTTOM
1m dia.
baffle wall
TWO inlets can be placed at convenient points along the circumference
PLAN X-X

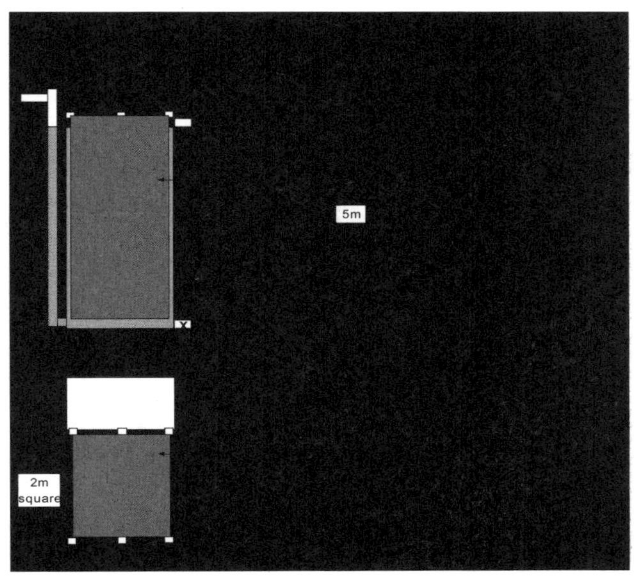

5m
2m square

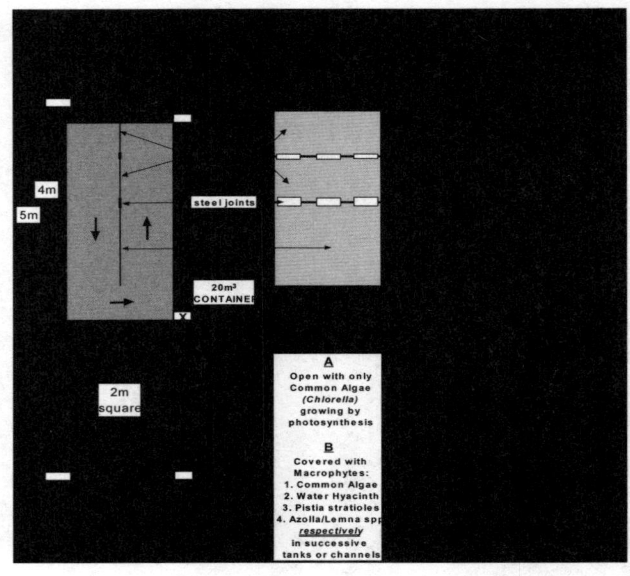

TANGIBLE BENEFITS
from the IBS :

- Big Quantity of FREE Feeds Available for Livestock

- Self-Sufficiency in Energy and Organic Fertilizers

- Self-Sufficiency in Planktonic Feeds for Fish and Shellfish

- Self-Sufficiency in Raw Materials for Agro-Industry

**NO Toxic Chemicals or Organic
Wastes to Degrade Environment**

- ## **ASSESSMENT of BENEFITS in the IBS**

- ## **THE INTEGRATED BIOMASS SYSTEM CAN REMOVE ALL CONSTRAINTS in the FARMS and AGRO-INDUSTRIES of MOST TROPICAL NATIONS by TOTAL RECYCLING of ALL WASTES & RESIDUES**

- ## **THE WASTES are COMPLETELY TREATED & THE BYPRODUCTS are FULLY REUTILIZED to GIVE ALL MEANS of PRODUCTION to FARMERS for MAXIMUM YIELDS at LOWEST COSTS**

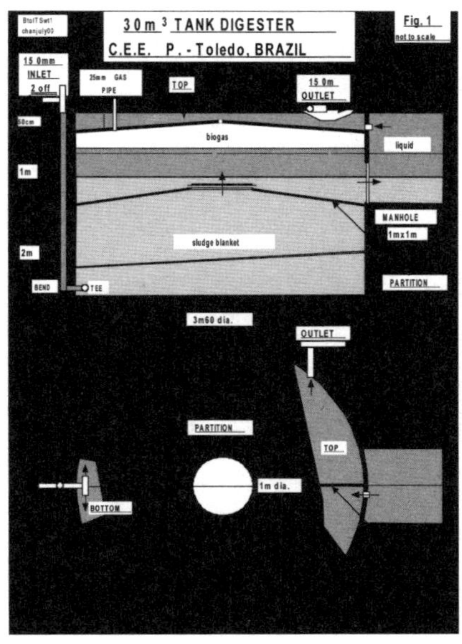

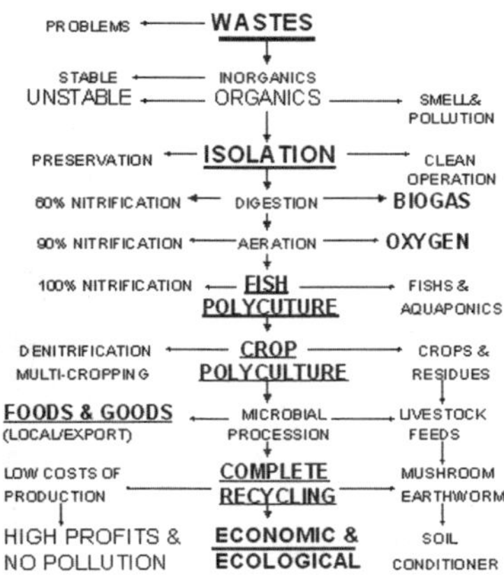

The FISH in turn produce a second cycle of WASTES, that are
naturally treated in the big pond, and the nutrients are used to
irrigate & fertilized crops on both water and dikes.

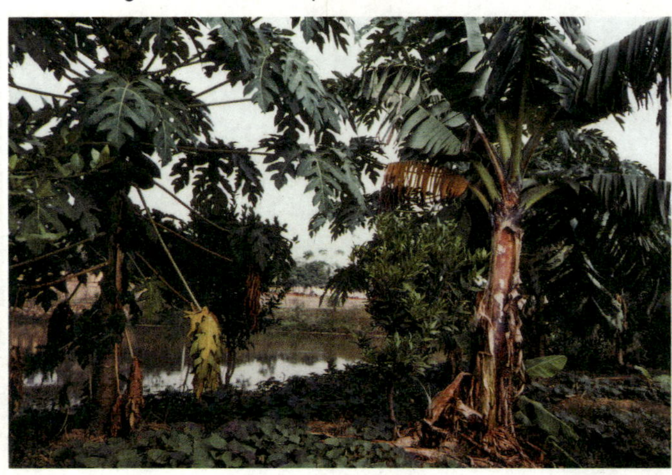

The DIKES have been enhanced with raising of chickens &
earthworms (as feeds) under the banana trees, with the chicken
wastes providing extra nutrients for the bananas.

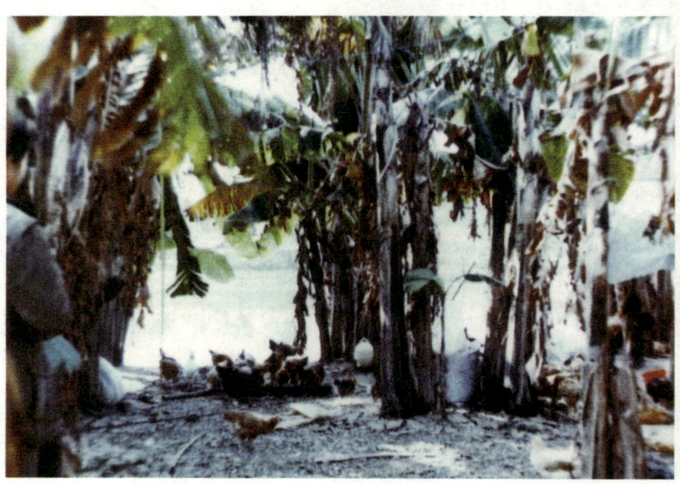

The dikes have mulberry bushes on half their area & their leaves
are used to feed silkworms for the silk industry.

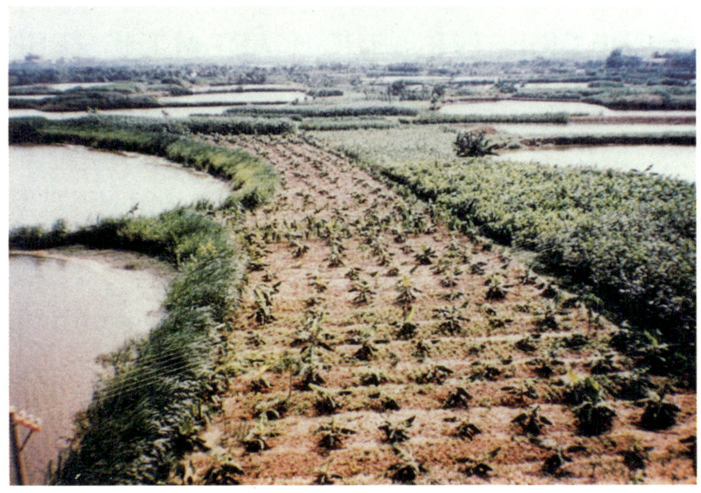

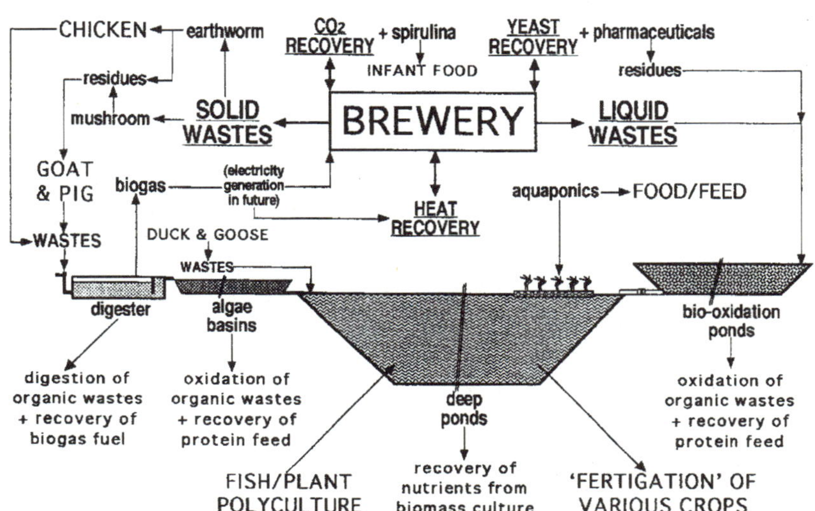

- ## **ROLES of DIGESTERS in WASTE RECYCLING**

- **THE DIGESTER is THE <u>HEART</u> of THE ZERI INTEGRATED BIOMASS SYSTEM WITH <u>ANAEROBIC PROCESSES</u>**

- **WITHOUT THE DIGESTER ALLTHE OTHER PROCESSES WILL TAKE <u>LONGER</u> and <u>NEITHER</u> be as EFFECTIVE NOR EFFICIENT**

- **THE DIGESTER CAN REMOVE OVER 60% of <u>BOD</u> and <u>COD</u> of THE INCOMING LIVESTOCK WASTES WITHIN 3 to 6 DAYS. With the Upflow Anaerobic Sludge Blanket (UASB), and more effective settling, the SAME results are obtained in LESS THAN ONE DAY**

Treatment of wastes is done in digesters, oxidation basins, big ponds, and crop fields

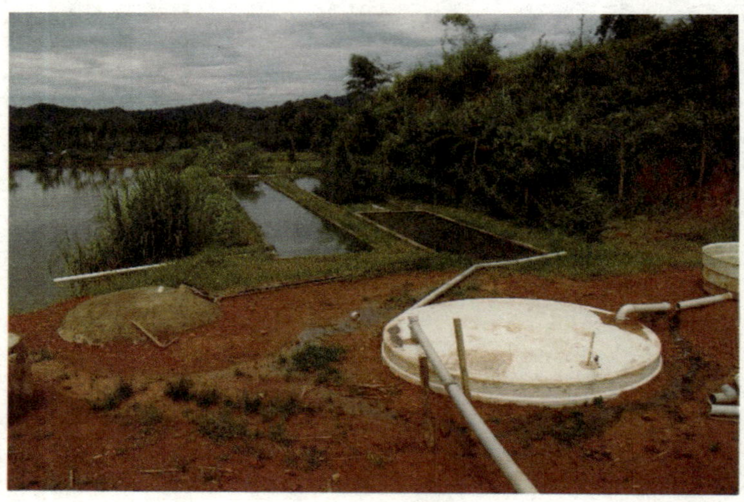

Harvesting natural algae as protein feed

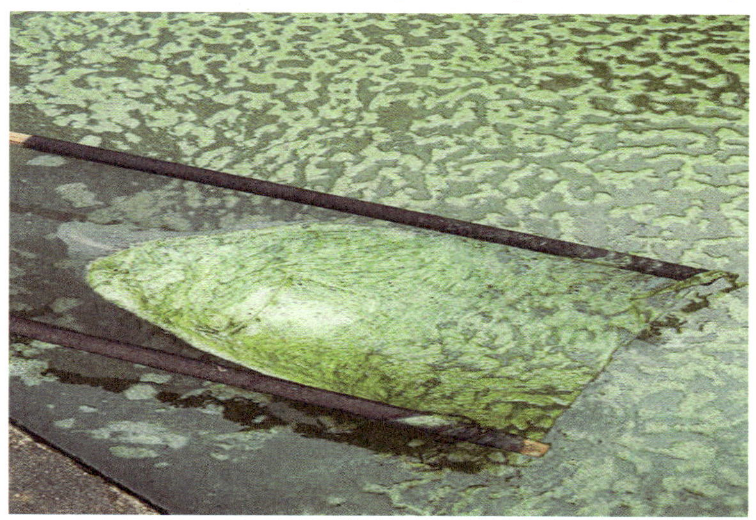

Shallow basins with natural algae, providing free oxygen

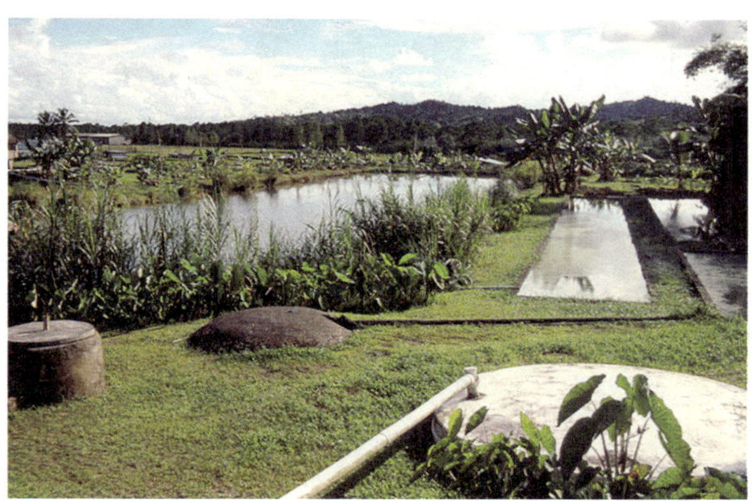

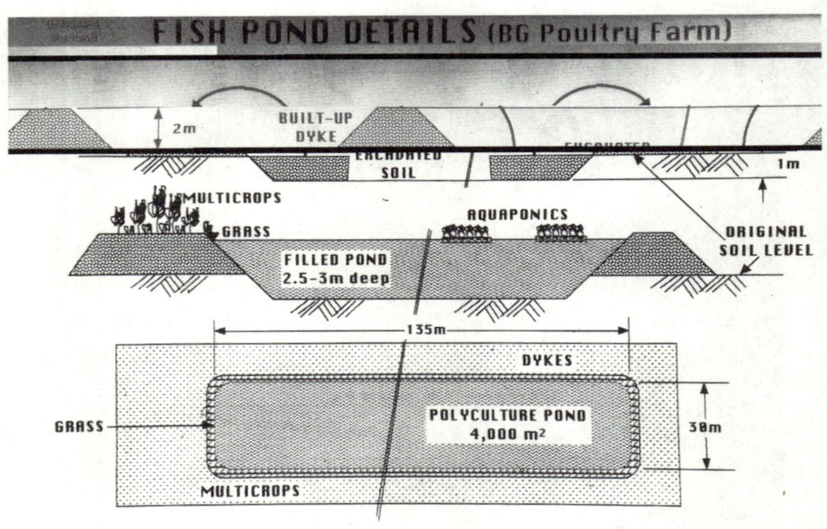

FISH POND DETAILS (BG Poultry Farm)
BUILT-UP DYKE
2m
EXCAVATED SOIL
EXCAVATED
1m
MULTICROPS
GRASS
AQUAPONICS
ORIGINAL SOIL LEVEL
FILLED POND
2.5–3m deep
135m
DYKES
GRASS
POLYCULTURE POND
4,000 m²
38m
MULTICROPS

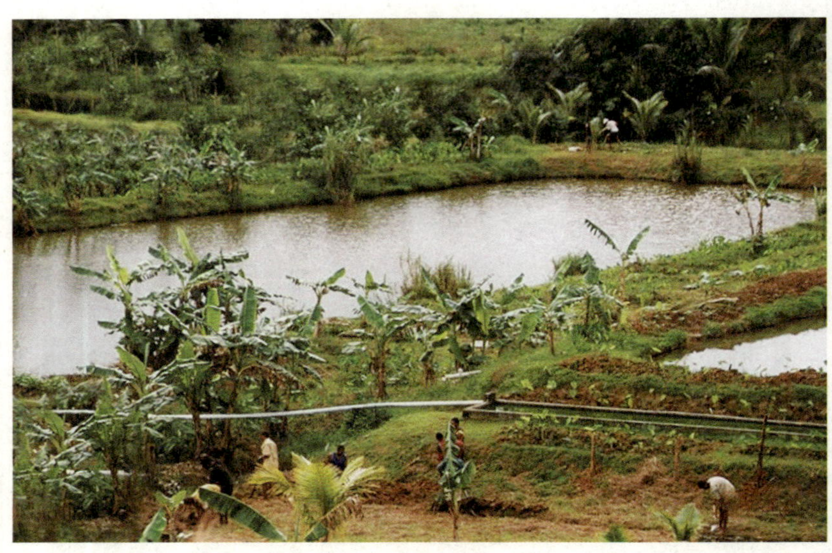

Deep pond for Polyculture of different kinds of fish.

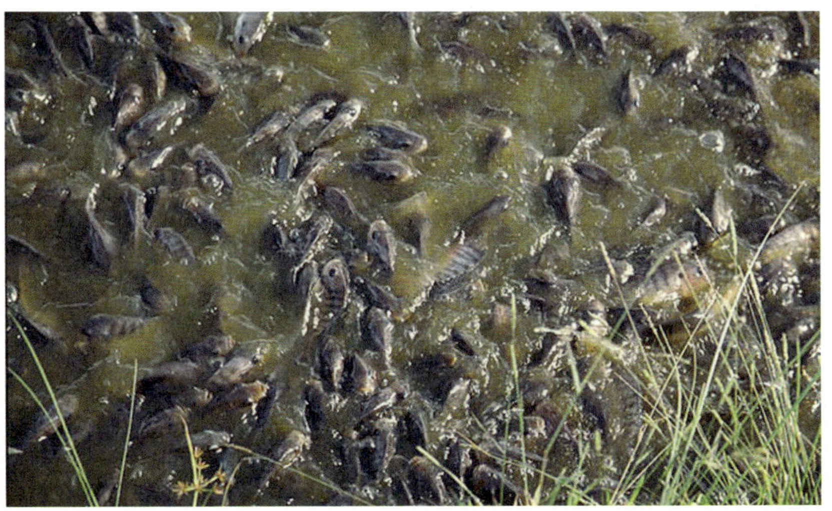

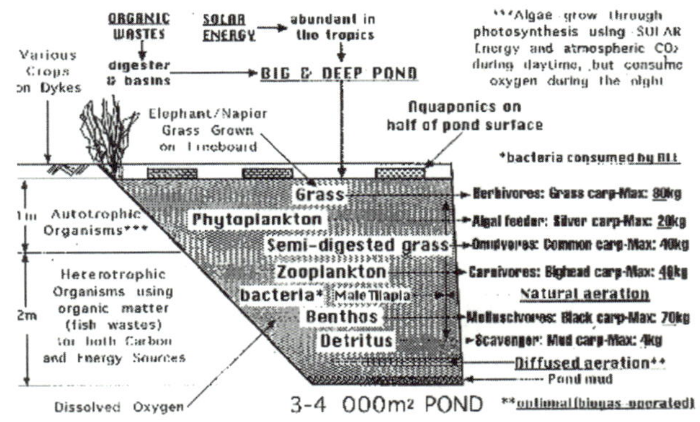

Macrophytes are grown abundantly to demineralise the effluent and used for cultures of high-value crops.

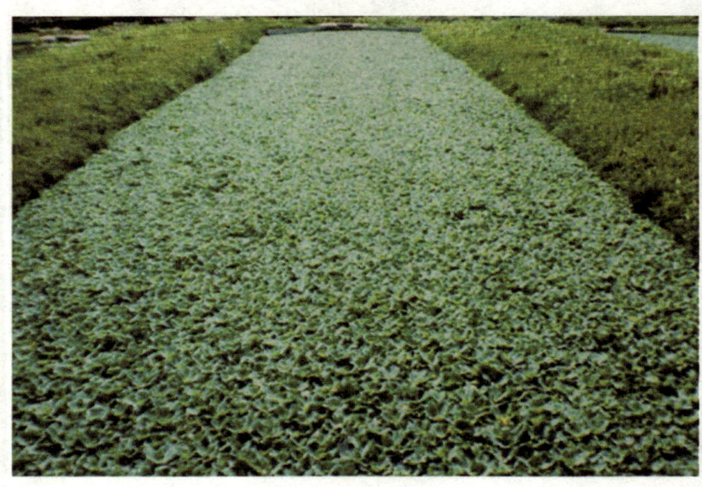

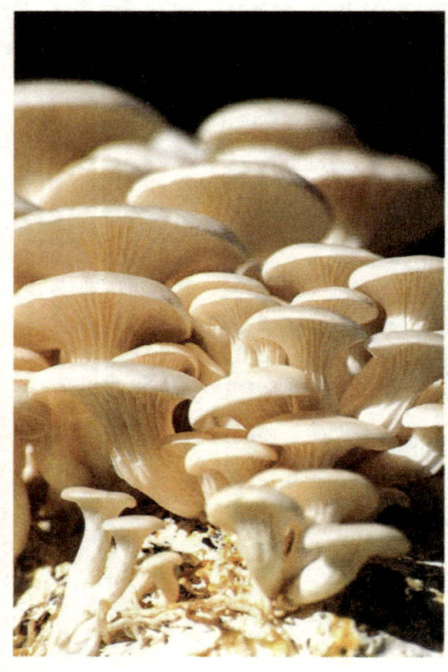

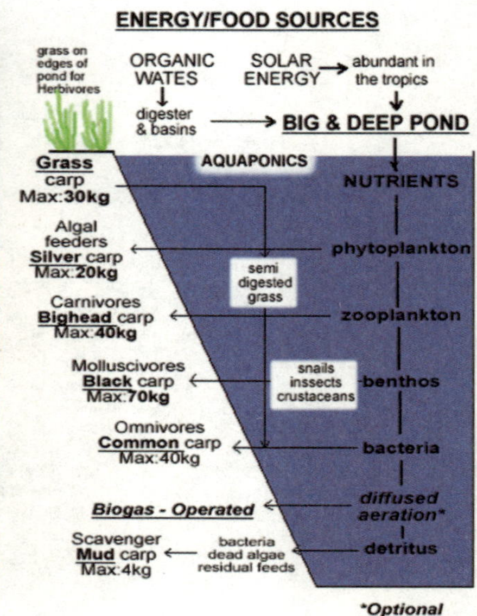

Substrate in bags is sterilized with free biogas

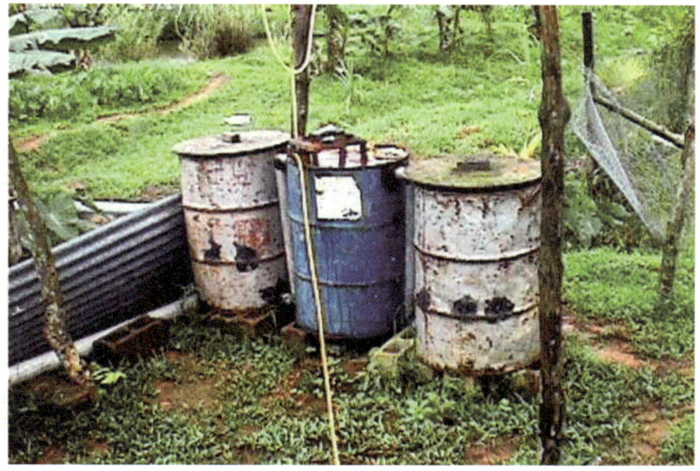

California red earthworms (Eisenia fetida) are cultivated on organic household GARBAGE from a family of four, and various fiber wastes, including shredded office paper.

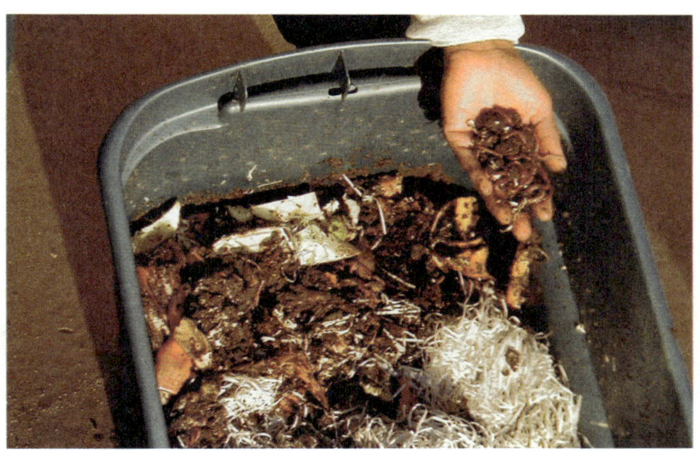

Sorghum Brewery in Namibia, South-Western Africa.

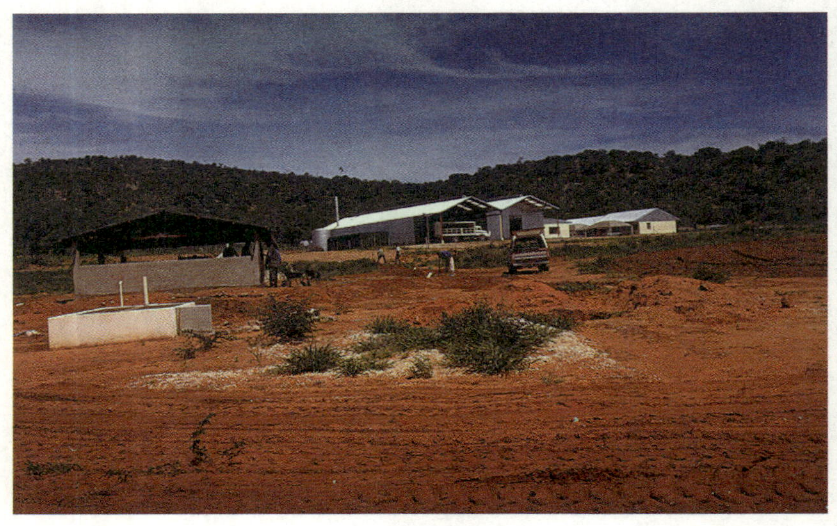

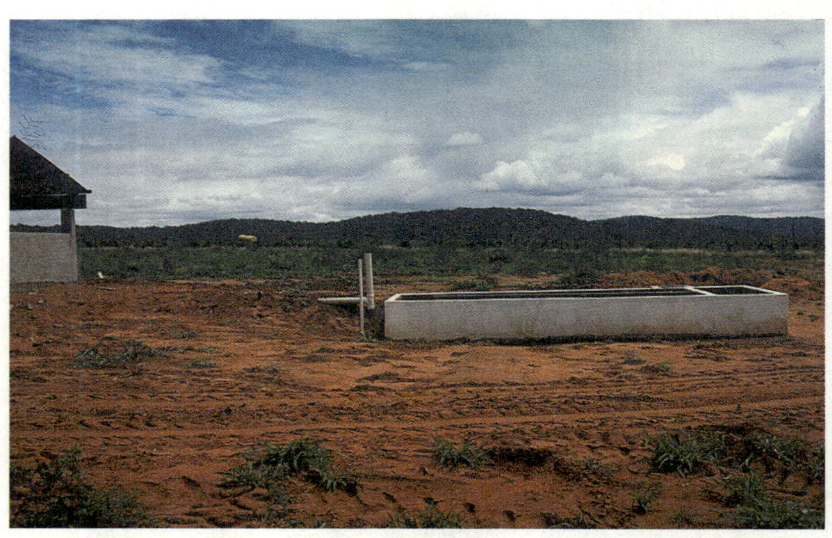

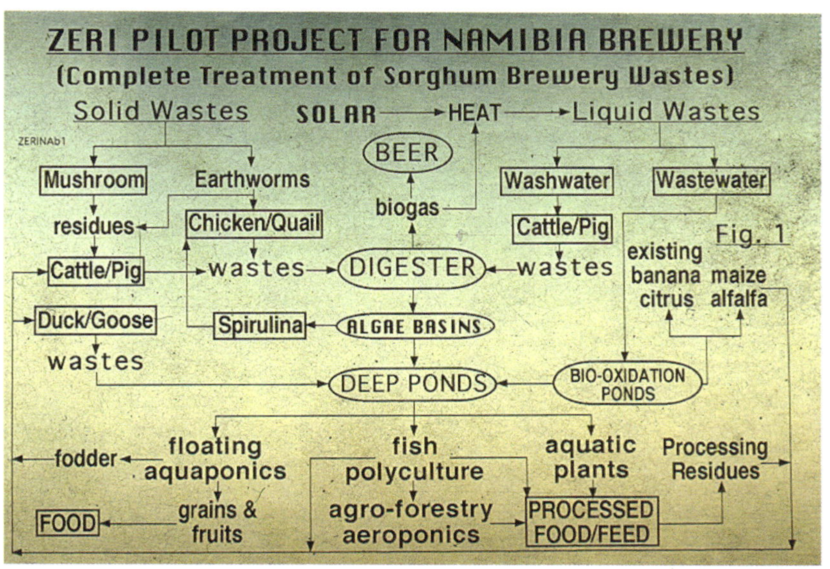

ZERI PILOT PROJECT FOR NAMIBIA BREWERY
(Complete Treatment of Sorghum Brewery Wastes)
Solid Wastes
SOLAR → HEAT → Liquid Wastes
ZERINAb1
BEER
Mushroom
Earthworms
Washwater
Wastewater
residues
Chicken/Quail
biogas
Cattle/Pig
Fig. 1
Cattle/Pig
wastes
DIGESTER
wastes
existing
banana
citrus
maize
alfalfa
Duck/Goose
Spirulina
ALGAE BASINS
wastes
DEEP PONDS
BIO-OXIDATION
PONDS
fodder
floating
aquaponics
fish
polyculture
aquatic
plants
Processing
Residues
FOOD
grains &
fruits
agro-forestry
aeroponics
PROCESSED
FOOD/FEED

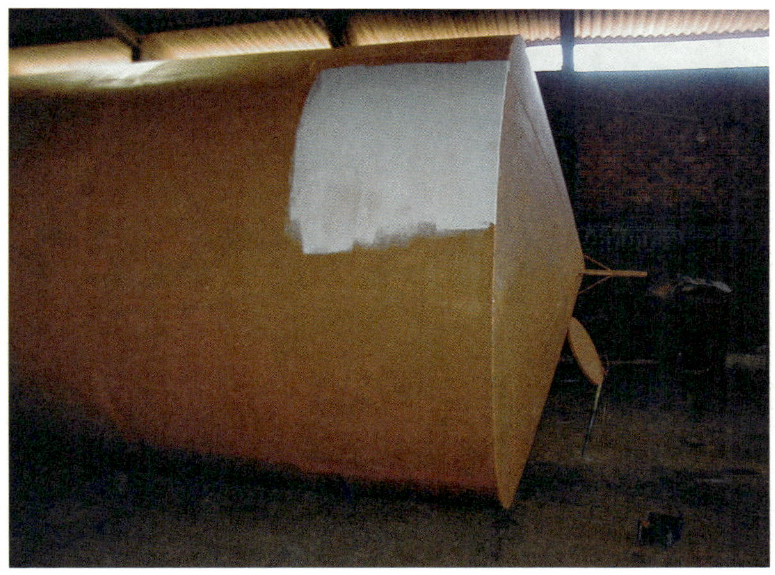

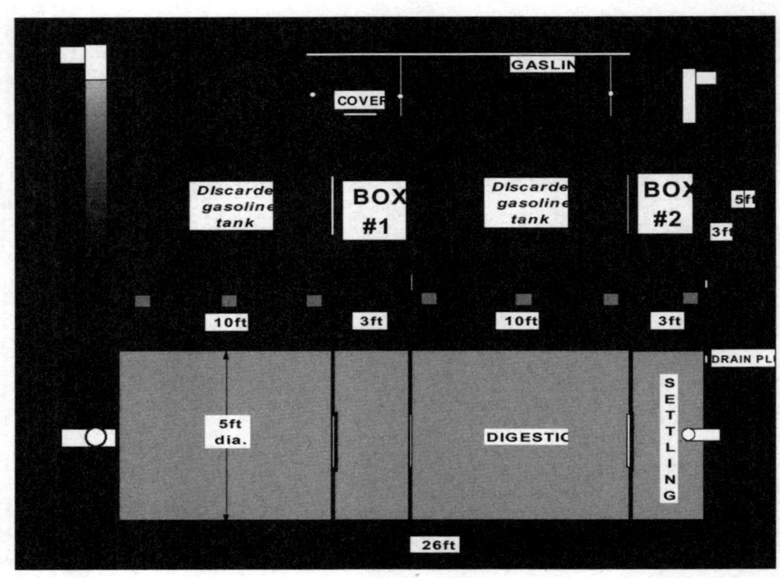
GASLIN
COVER
Discarde
gasoline
tank
BOX
#1
Discarde
gasoline
tank
BOX
#2
5ft
3ft
10ft
3ft
10ft
3ft
DRAIN PL
5ft
dia.
DIGESTIC
SETTLING
26ft

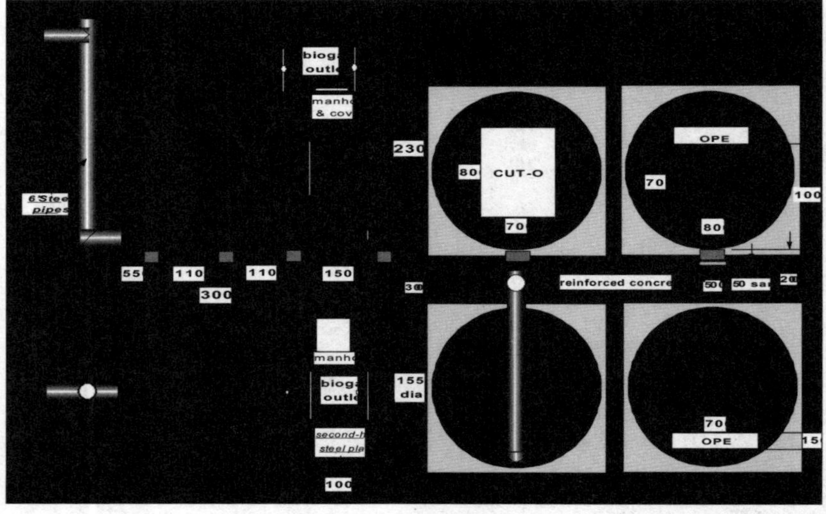
bioga
outle
manh
& cov
230
6'Stee
pipes
80
CUT-O
OPE
70
100
70
80
55
110
110
150
3
reinforced concre
50
50 sa
2
300
manh
biog
outle
155
dia
70
OPE
15
second-h
steel pla
100

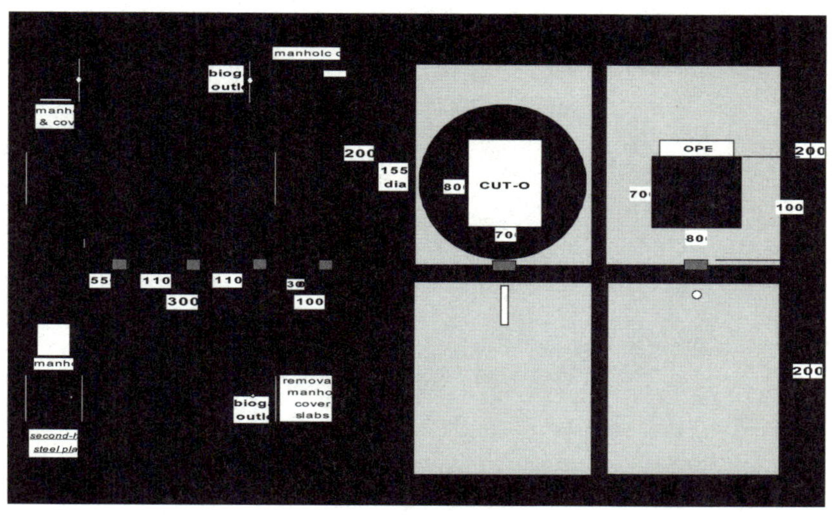

manhole cover
biog
outle
manhole
& cov
200
155
dia
800
CUT-O
700
OPE
700
200
100
800
55
110
110
300
300
100
200
manho
remova
manho
cover
slabs
biog
outle
second-h
steel pla

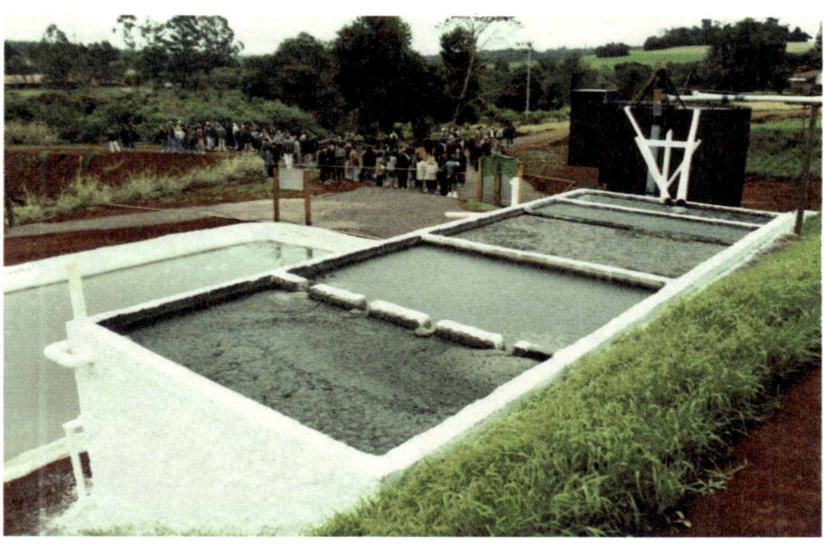

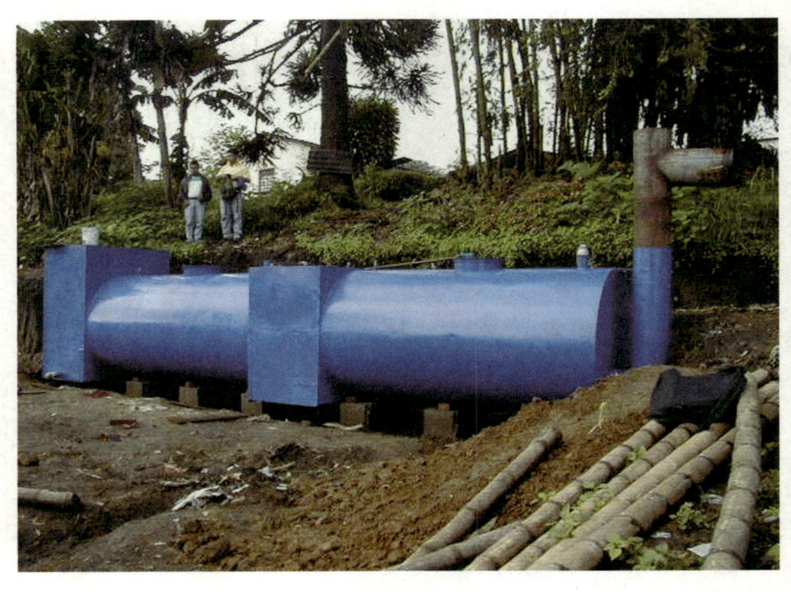

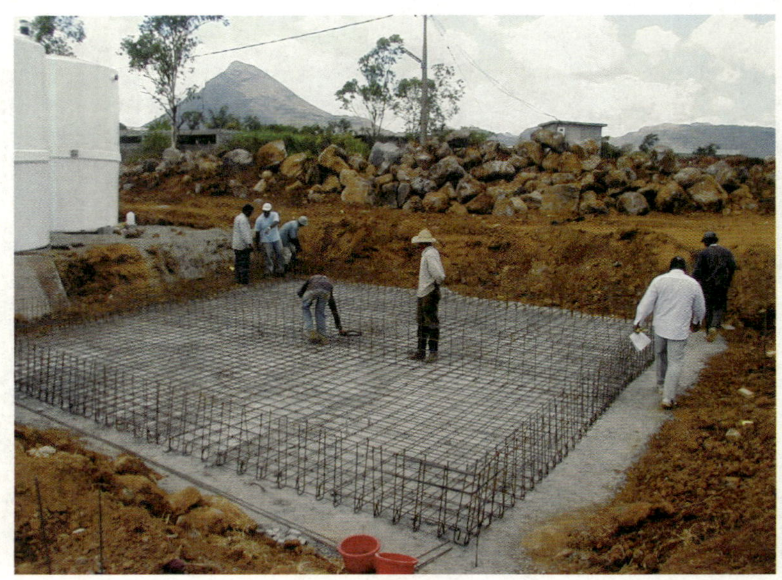

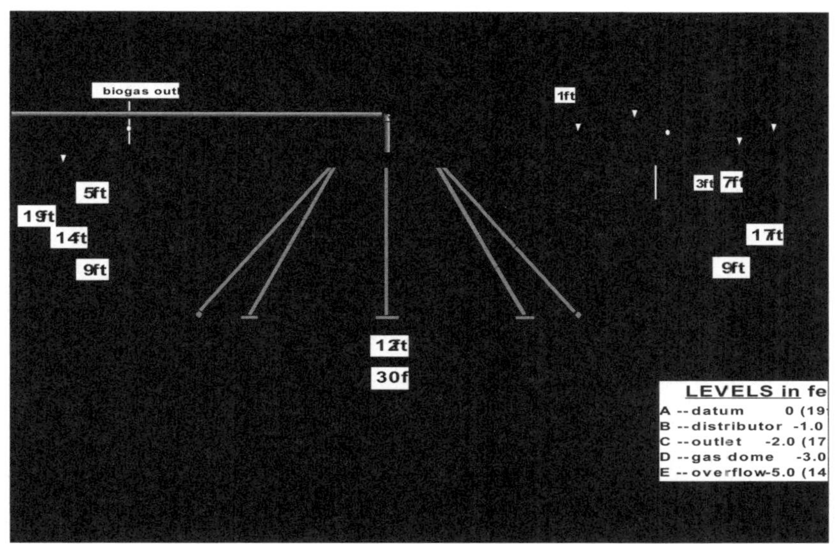

biogas out
1ft
5ft
19ft
14ft
9ft
3ft 7ft
17ft
9ft
12ft
30f
LEVELS in fe
A -- datum   0 (19
B -- distributor -1.0
C -- outlet   -2.0 (17
D -- gas dome   -3.0
E -- overflow -5.0 (14

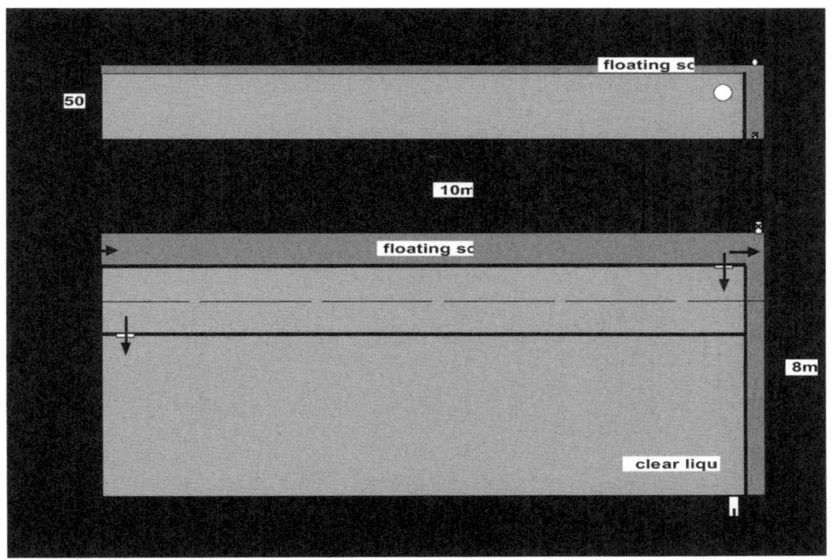

floating sc
50
10m
floating sc
clear liqu
8m

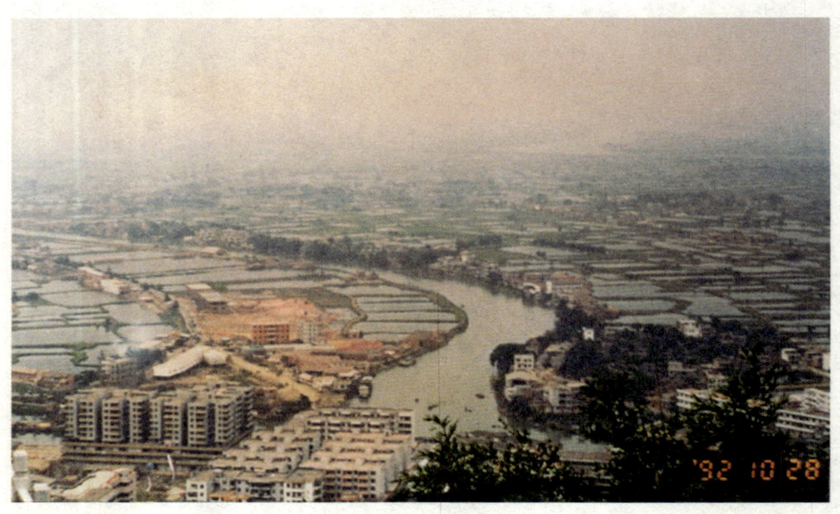

'92 10 28

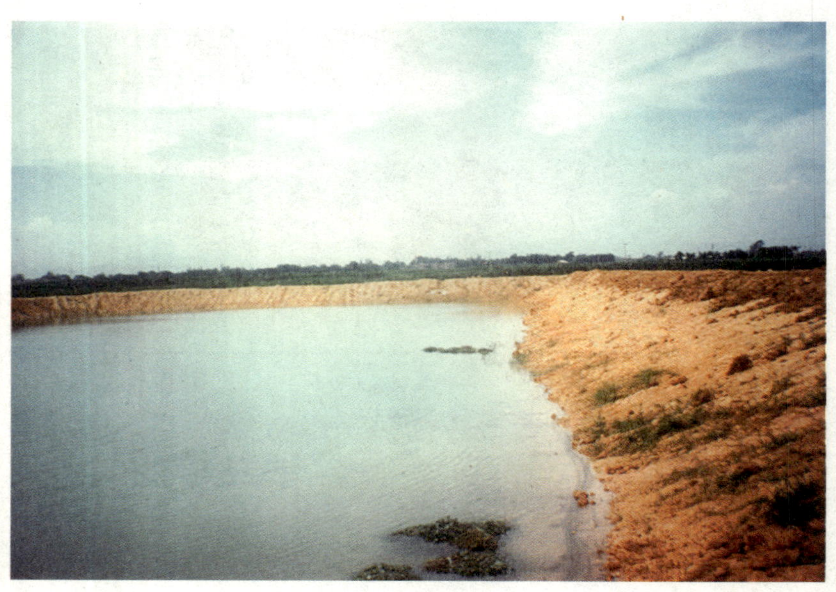

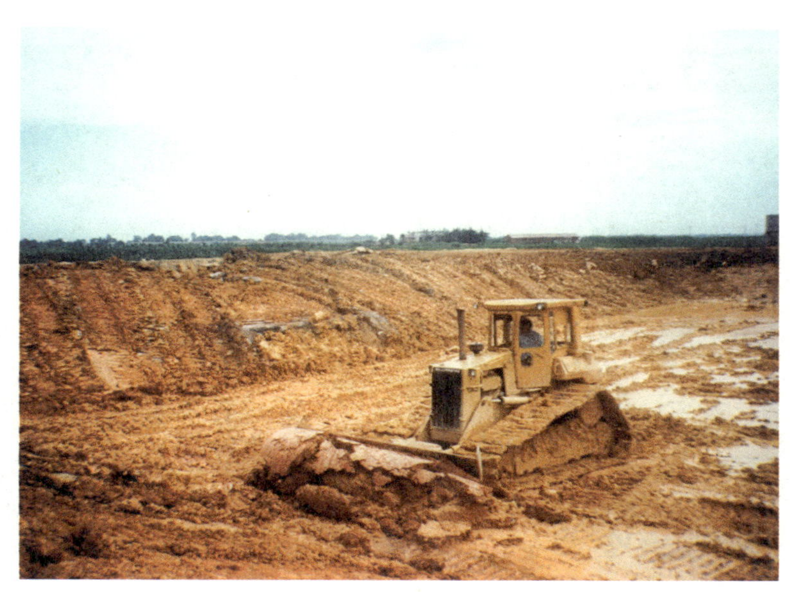

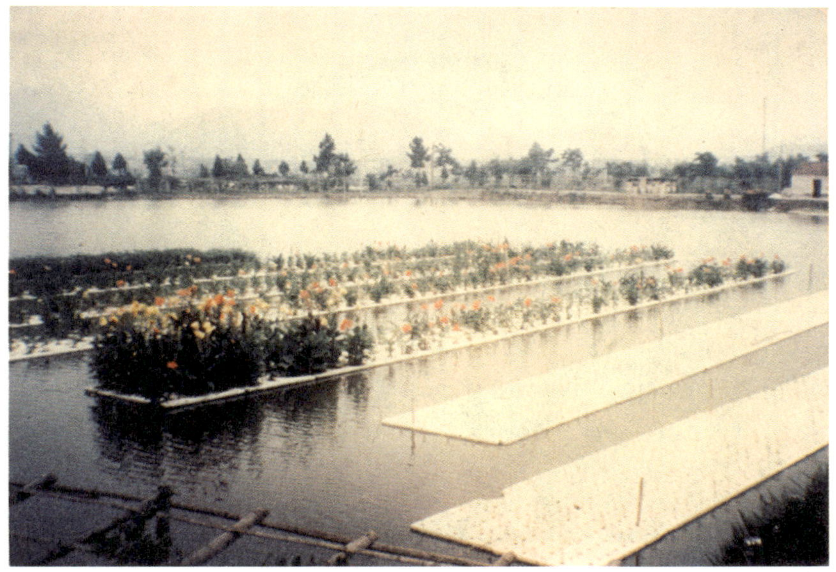

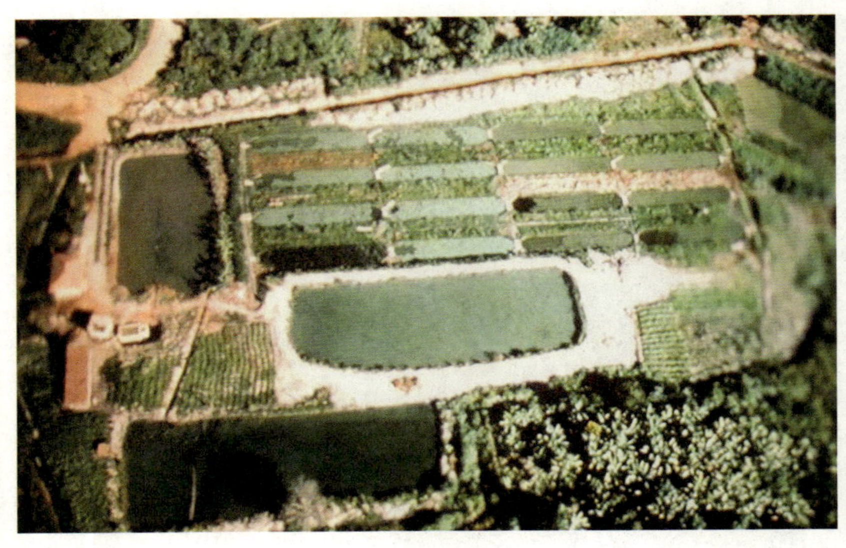

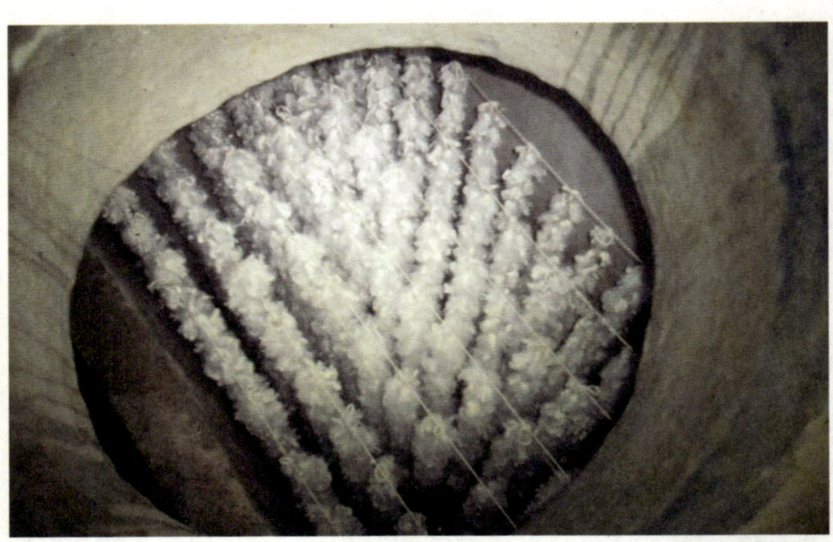

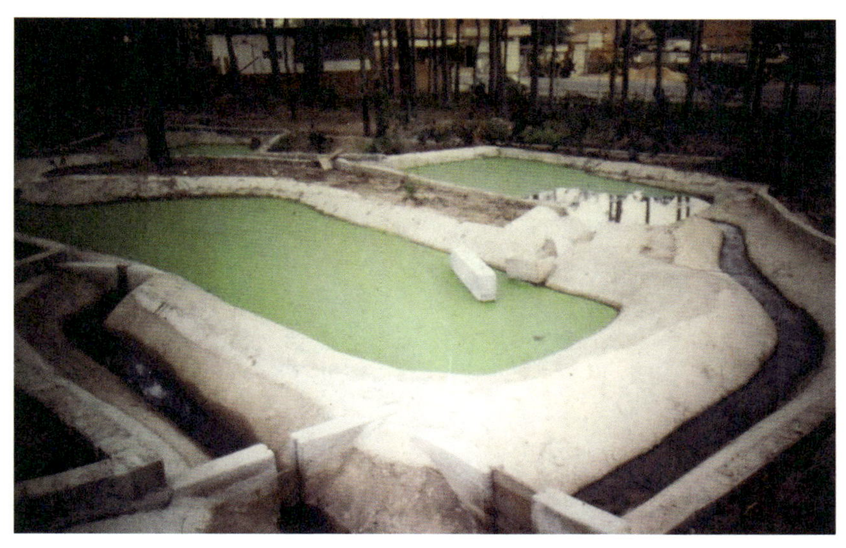

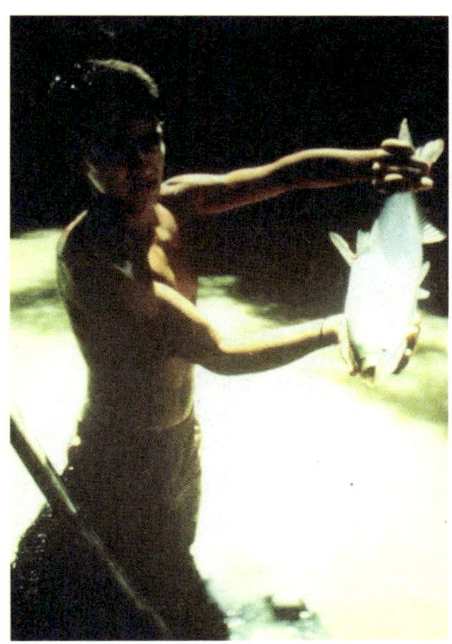

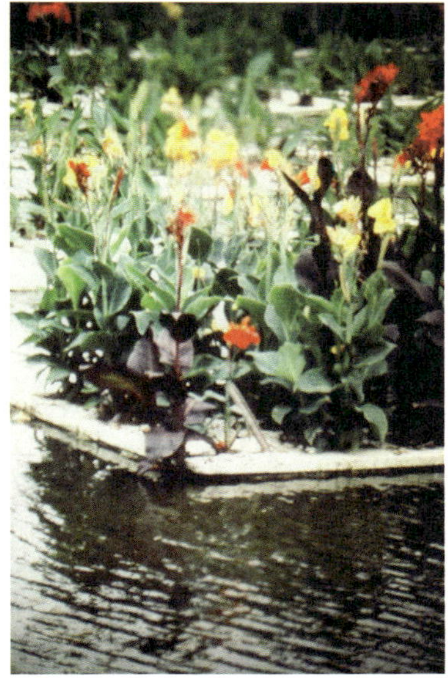

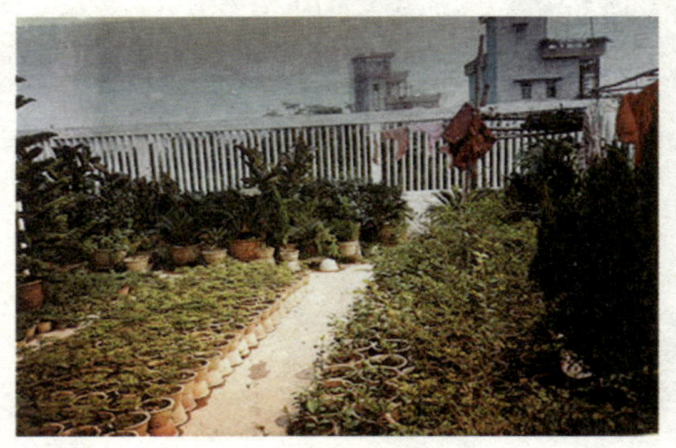

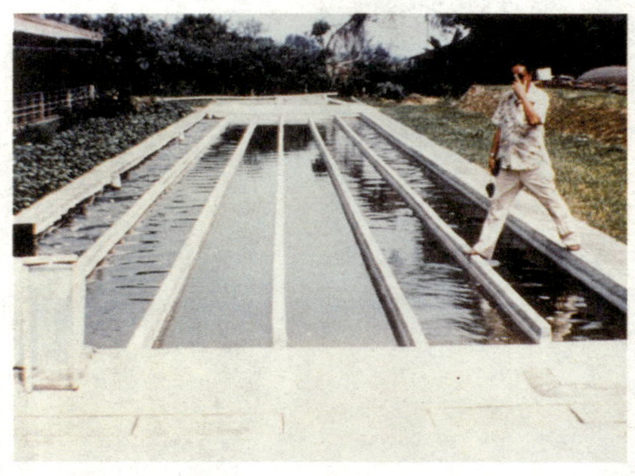

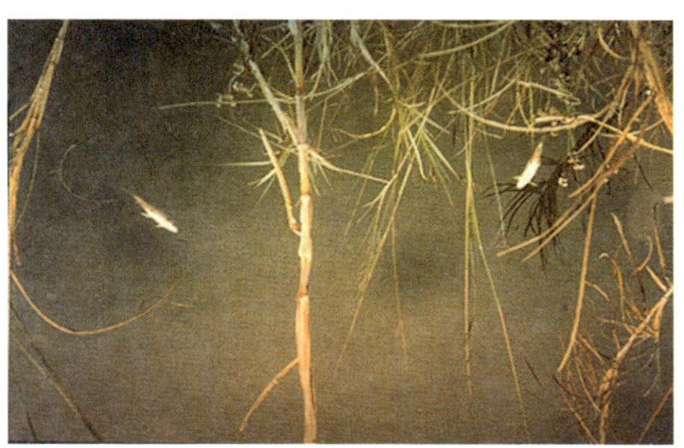

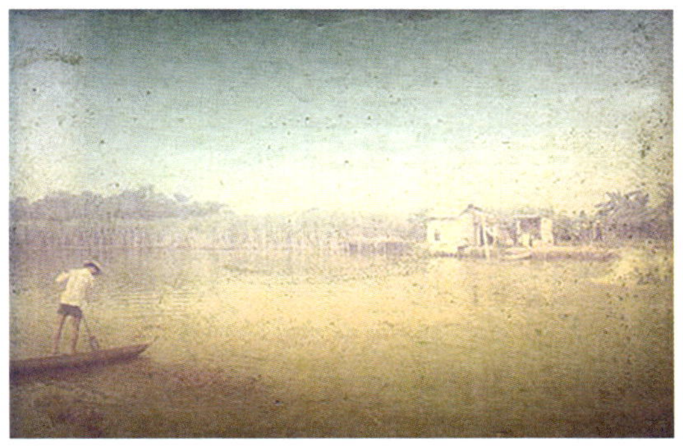

100 Notes – 100 Thoughts / 100 Notizen – 100 Gedanken

№051: George Chan
Dream Farms / Traumfarmen
Introduction / Einführung: Fernando García-Dory

dOCUMENTA (13), 9/6/2012 – 16/9/2012
Artistic Director / Künstlerische Leiterin: Carolyn Christov-Bakargiev
Member of Core Agent Group, Head of Department /
Mitglied der Agenten-Kerngruppe, Leiterin der Abteilung: Chus Martínez
Head of Publications / Leiterin der Publikationsabteilung: Bettina Funcke

Managing Editor / Redaktion und Lektorat: Katrin Sauerländer
Editorial Assistant / Redaktionsassistentin: Cordelia Marten
English Copyediting / Englisches Lektorat: Melissa Larner
English Proofreading / Englisches Korrektorat: Sam Frank
Translation / Übersetzung: Nikolaus G. Schneider
Graphic Design and Typesetting / Grafische Gestaltung und Satz: Leftloft
Typeface / Schrift: Glypha, Plantin
Production / Verlagsherstellung: Christine Emter
Reproductions / Reproduktionen: weyhing digital, Ostfildern
Paper / Papier: Pop'Set, 240 g/m², Munken Print Cream 15, 90 g/m²
Manufacturing / Gesamtherstellung: Dr. Cantz'sche Druckerei, Ostfildern

© 2011 documenta und Museum Fridericianum Veranstaltungs-GmbH, Kassel;
Hatje Cantz Verlag, Ostfildern; George Chan; Fernando García-Dory

Illustrations / Abbildungen: p. / S. 1: Students on deck of Chalet III (Farrally Hall) /
Studenten auf der Terrasse des Chalet III (Farrally Hall), The Banff Centre, 1956
(detail / Detail), courtesy Paul D. Fleck Library & Archives at The Banff Centre;
all other illustrations / alle anderen Abbildungen: © George Chan

documenta und Museum Fridericianum
Veranstaltungs-GmbH
Friedrichsplatz 18, 34117 Kassel
Germany / Deutschland
Tel. +49 561 70727-0
Fax +49 561 70727-39
www.documenta.de
Chief Executive Officer / Geschäftsführer: Bernd Leifeld

Published by / Erschienen im
Hatje Cantz Verlag
Zeppelinstrasse 32, 73760 Ostfildern
Germany / Deutschland
Tel. +49 711 4405-200
Fax +49 711 4405-220
www.hatjecantz.com

ISBN 978-3-7757-2900-0 (Print)
ISBN 978-3-7757-3080-8 (E-Book)

Printed in Germany

Gefördert durch die

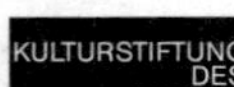

funded by the German Federal
Cultural Foundation